Lizards
COLORING BOOK

JAN SOVAK

DOVER PUBLICATIONS, INC.
MINEOLA, NEW YORK

Note

Lizards are reptiles of the order Squamata, which they share with snakes. Both lizards and snakes probably originated in the Triassic era, some 200 million years ago. Although some lizards closely resemble snakes, lizards are different in that they usually have four legs, external ear openings, and movable eyelids. Nevertheless, there are legless lizards, such as the Eastern Glass Lizard, that are easily confused with snakes.

Today roughly 3,000 species of lizards are found in the world, ranging in size from tiny two-inch Caribbean geckos to the fearsome ten-foot Komodo Dragon. Like other reptiles, lizards lay eggs, although some are capable of live births. They are also cold-blooded, meaning that their body temperature varies with the outside atmosphere. Despite lacking an internal heat source, however, lizards have colonized almost all environments except Antarctica.

Among the special characteristics of lizards is the ability of some types to break off their tails (usually to escape from predators) and grow new ones. In addition, certain species, such as the anole and chameleon, are able to change color in response to the environment, or when alarmed, enabling them to instantly camouflage themselves from their enemies.

This book contains detailed, accurate drawings of thirty different lizards, with identifying captions. Each caption contains a brief description of the species, with specific information on the lizard's coloration to help insure accurate coloring.

Bibliographical Note

Lizards Coloring Book is a new work, first published by Dover Publications, Inc., in 2006.

DOVER *Pictorial Archive* SERIES

International Standard Book Number
ISBN-13: 978-0-486-44820-6
ISBN-10: 0-486-44820-7

Manufactured in the United States of America
Dover Publications, Inc., 31 East 2nd Street, Mineola, N.Y. 11501

Bearded Dragon (*Pogona vitticeps*). Native to central Australia, the bearded dragon is a stocky lizard that grows up to two feet in length, including tail. It features prominent spines along its sides and a spiny jaw pouch, which it puffs out like a black beard when it is frightened. This species ranges in color from pale to dark gray, with white elongated spots edged with black.

Blue-tailed Day Gecko (*Phelsuma cepediana*). This tree-dwelling gecko, found in Madagascar and Mauritius, has a blue-green body with reddish-brown spots, and a blue tail. Each foot has 5,000 tiny hairs, less than one-tenth the diameter of a human hair, called setae. These setae, each tipped with hundreds of microscopic spatula-shaped structures, help the gecko cling to walls, ceilings—almost any surface.

Blue-tongued Skink *(Tiliqua scincoides)*. Named for its long, blue tongue, this Australian lizard also possesses small legs, and a tail that can break off and regrow. Reaching a length of about two feet, the blue-tongued skink has dark, scaly skin with tan and gray/brown bands, pale tan legs and undersides. It eats insects, worms, snails, flowers, fruits, and berries.

Chuckwalla *(Sauromalus ater)*. Found in rocky, desert areas of the American Southwest, this large plump lizard eats fruit, leaves, buds, and flowers. Males have a black head, forelegs, and upper trunk, which is reddish-yellow toward the rear. When the chuckwalla senses danger, it wedges itself into a rocky crevice and inflates its body to deter predators.

Collared Lizard *(Crotaphytus collaris)*. The state lizard of Oklahoma, the collared lizard is noted for running upright on its hind legs, giving the appearance of a miniature Tyrannosaurus Rex. Reaching a length of twelve inches, its body is green, with prominent black bands behind the head, which may be bright yellow. In males the throat is brightly colored, and can be blue, green, or even orange.

Common Wall Lizard *(Podarcis muralis).* Found in mainland Europe and the United States, this small, thin lizard prefers urban settings where it can hide amidst rock, rubble, debris, and buildings. It is highly variable in color and pattern, but is generally brown or grayish, occasionally tinged with green. The tail is brown, gray, or rust in color.

6

Dabb Spiny-tailed Lizard (*Uromastyx acanthinurus*). This interesting, unusual lizard is native to northeastern Africa. It deters predators with its strong jaws and spiny tail, often blocking the entrance to its burrow or crevice with its massive tail. Coloration ranges from dark brown to gray or black, with yellow, white, or orange markings on the back.

Double-Crested Basilisk (*Basiliscus plumifrons*). Green with white spots, this twenty-inch-long lizard may be found in the Caribbean lowlands from Nicaragua to Panama. Its rapid speed and the formation of air pockets around its feet enable it to run a short distance across water. The male has well-developed crests on its head, body, and tail.

Dwarf Flat Lizard *(Platysaurus guttatus)*. At home in the arid savannas of Africa, this lizard is very agile, and is found in small family groups on isolated rocky outcrops. Adult males are green to blue-green, with numerous pale spots, and three pale stripes on the head. The tail is bright orange, while the throat is pale green with black specks.

Eastern Glass Lizard *(Ophisaurus ventralis)*. Often mistaken for snakes, these long, legless lizards inhabit wet meadows, sand dunes, and coastal forests of the southeastern United States. (Unlike snakes, lizards have eyelids and ear openings.) Growing up to forty-three inches in length, adult lizards are black with square green spots and yellow bellies.

Fijian Crested Iguana (*Brachylophus vitiensis*). First discovered in 1979, this large, stocky lizard is named for the distinct crest of spines along its back. Its body is green, with narrow white bands across the upper surface. When alarmed it can change color very rapidly, from green to black. A vegetarian, this iguana is especially partial to hibiscus flowers.

Frill-necked Lizard (*Chlamydosaurus kingii*). Found in Australia and New Guinea, the frill-necked lizard is named for the frill that normally lies in folds around its shoulders and neck. When the lizard is frightened, this frill expands into an umbrella shape around the head, displaying a round broad expanse of orange and red scales meant to deter predators. These lizards may be gray, brown, or reddish-brown.

Giant Monitor Lizard (*Varanus giganteus*). The largest Australian monitor lizard, this fearsome predator can be up to eight feet in length. Its upper surfaces are brown or black, with rows of light-colored spots on its back and tail. Inhabiting arid, rocky terrain, the giant monitor lizard eats snakes, lizards, birds, and small mammals—even small kangaroos.

Gila Monster (*Heloderma suspectum*). One of only two species of venomous lizards (the other is the Mexican bearded lizard), the gila monster inhabits the deserts of the southwestern United States. Full-grown lizards may be two feet in length, with stout bodies, and a strong, tenacious bite. They have black faces, and black, orange, pink or yellow broken blotches on their bodies.

14

Gliding Gecko (*Ptychozoon kuhli*). Native to southeast Asia, this nocturnal lizard feeds on crickets, locusts, and worms. These geckos have webbed feet and frills on their cheeks, tails, and flanks. When the frills are extended, the lizards can glide through the air. Gliding geckos are dark gray or brown, with orange markings on the back.

Granite Night Lizard *(Xantusia henshawi)*. These California lizards have flat bodies, with broad, flat heads and soft skin. Secretive and hard to find, they are small creatures (1¼" to 2¾" long) with rounded dark dorsal spots on a pale yellow or cream background.

16

Green Anole *(Anolis carolinensis)*. A tree-dwelling lizard native to the southeastern United States and the Caribbean, the green anole has special pads on its feet that enable it to climb, cling, and run on almost any surface.

In addition, it has a large pink fan of skin on its neck, called a dewlap, which the anole extends for courtship or territorial display.

17

Green Iguana (*Iguana iguana*). Found in the tropical rain forests of Central and South America, the green iguana can reach a length of six feet. Its rough skin ranges from bright green to a dull grayish-green, with a set of pointy scales along its back. The iguana's long fingers and claws help it to climb and to grasp its prey.

Jackson's Chameleon (*Chameleon jacksonii*). These lime-green tree-dwelling lizards are found in Africa and Madagascar at elevations of five to seven thousand feet. The males possess three horns used in "shoving" matches with rivals. Jackson's chameleons have independently focusing eyes, which can swivel in different directions, giving the lizards 360 degrees vision.

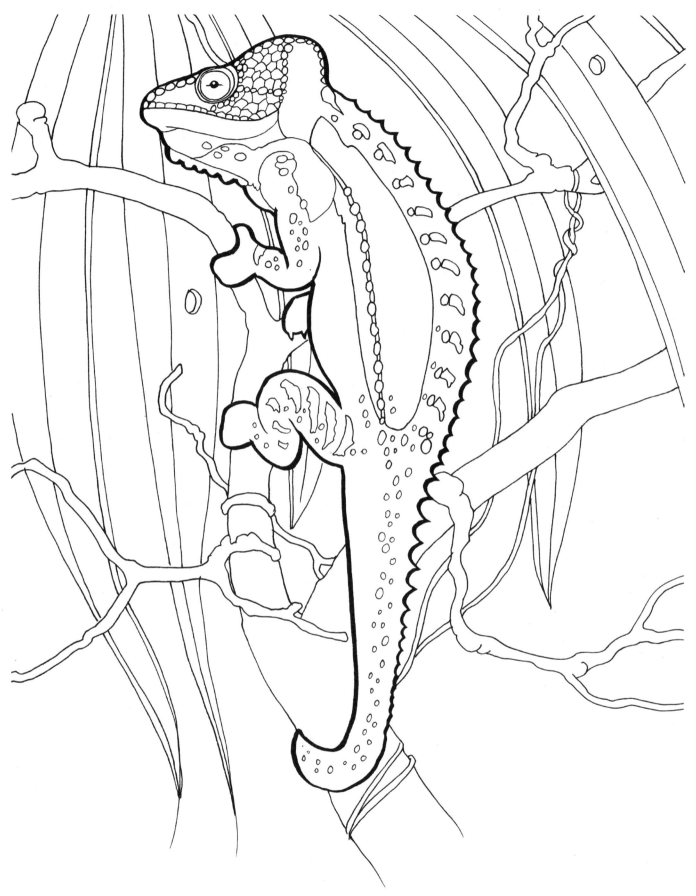

Knysna Dwarf Chameleon *(Bradypodion damaranum)*. Native to Africa, this small (up to seven inches) chameleon lives in wet coastal areas, feeding on insects at night. Its coloring is an intense green, turquoise or blue shade, with a long yellow, orange, red, or purple spot on its sides.

Komodo Dragon *(Varanus komodensis)*. The world's largest lizard, growing up to ten feet in length, this giant monitor lizard is found mainly on the Indonesian islands of Komodo, Rintja, Padar, and Flores. Swift runners and climbers, Komodo dragons are ferocious predators with an appetite for deer and wild boar. Their coloration ranges from gray and brown, to reddish-brown, with yellowish marks on the head and neck. This dragon has a foot-long, yellow forked tongue.

Leaf-tailed Gecko (*Uroplatus fimbriatus*). Tree-dwelling and nocturnal, the leaf-tailed gecko lives in Madagascar, where it hunts at night for spiders, cockroaches, and other prey. This gecko gets its name from its large, leaf-shaped tail, which can break off and regrow. This lizard also relies largely on its superb green and brown camouflage—it blends in with bark, moss, and lichens—to protect it from predators.

22

Marine Iguana *(Amblyrhyncus cristatus)*. Although they look fearsome, these lizards, native to the Galapagos Islands, are harmless vegetarians. Feeding mainly on seaweed, they are black in color, sometimes with blotches of coppery green and red on their backs. Marine iguanas grow up to four feet in length, and possess long sharp claws that help them cling to rocks in rough seas.

Ocellated Lizard (*Lacerta lepida*). Native to Spain, this blue-spotted green reptile grows to twenty inches or longer. It dwells in stone walls, rock piles, and rabbit holes, and eats mainly insects, but also other lizards, small mammals, birds' eggs, and fruit.

Regal Horned Lizard (*Phrynosoma solare*). Named for the horns protruding from the back of its head, this denizen of the Arizona deserts feeds on beetles and ants, which it captures with its sticky tongue. Coloration ranges from tan to reddish-brown to gray, and the lizard's flattened body is fringed with a row of spines.

Rhinoceros Iguana *(Cyclura cornuta)*. The horny out-growths on the end of its nose gave this lizard its name. Dusky gray or olive-green, the rhinoceros iguana is found in the Caribbean where it spends much of its time in underground burrows or dens. It is a powerful lizard, up to two-and-a-half feet long, which mainly eats leaves and fruit, but also preys on insects, worms, crabs, and mice.

Sail-tailed Lizard *(Hydrosaurus pustulosus)*. This rare, river-dwelling lizard of eastern Indonesia is named for the sail-like appendage on its tail. Resembling a dinosaur, the sail-tailed lizard is bluish-black, with yellow markings on its sides and under the throat. In addition, it sports a row of spines along its back.

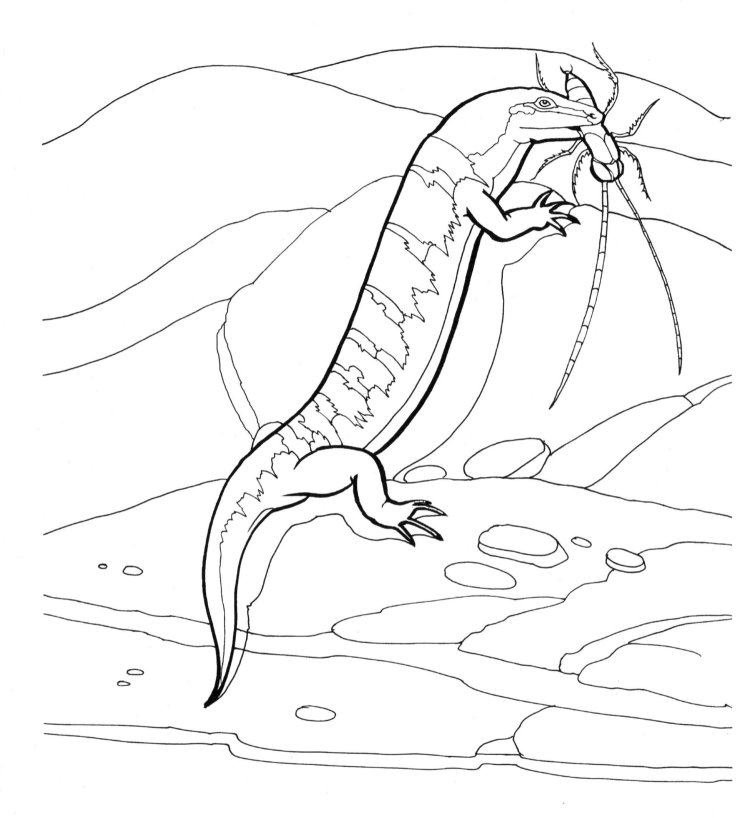

Sand Skink (*Scincus scincus* spp.). Inhabiting deserts from North Africa to Iran, the sand skink has a broad, thick body, with small legs and feet. This species is active during the day, and is adept at digging, disappearing rapidly in loose sand when frightened. The skink's coloration is yellowish to light brown, with dark bands.

Sun Gazer *(Cordylus giganteus)*. Resembling a baby alligator, the sun gazer inhabits the grasslands of South Africa. Its defensive weapons include sharp, pointed scales on the neck and tail. In addition, when the sun gazer is threatened, it retreats into its burrow and blocks the entrance with its heavily armored tail. These lizards have dark brown backs and lighter flanks (sometimes orange-tan).

Western Banded Gecko (*Coleonyx variegatus)*. Abundant in the deserts of the western United States, this nocturnal lizard avoids the heat of the day and hunts insects, spiders, and baby scorpions at night. Adults are pale yellow or light gray with red-brown spots on top of the head and red-brown bands across the back. Like other geckos, their tails can break off and grow back.